THE
LIGHT
ON
CHANTRY
ISLAND

National Library of Canada Cataloguing in Publication Data

Weeks-Mifflin, Mary
    The light on Chantry Island

Bibliography: p.
ISBN 0-919783-45-7

1. Lighthouses, Ontario — Southampton — History.
2, Chantry Island (Ont.) — History. 3. Southampton
(Ont.) — History. I Mifflin, Ray, 1950– II. Title

VR1027.05W44 1986   623.89'42'0971321   C86-093962-6

A BOSTON MILLS PRESS BOOK

PUBLISHED BY BOSTON MILLS PRESS
132 Main Street, Erin, Ontario N0B 1T0
Tel: 519-833-2407
Fax: 519-833-2195
e-mail: books@bostonmillspress.com
www.bostonmillspress.com

IN CANADA:
Distributed by Firefly Books Ltd.
3680 Victoria Park Avenue
Toronto, Ontario M2H 3K1

IN THE UNITED STATES:
Distributed by Firefly Books (U.S.) Inc.
P.O. Box 1338, Ellicott Station
Buffalo, New York 14205

Printed in Canada

THE LIGHT ON CHANTRY ISLAND

Mary Weeks-Mifflin & Ray Mifflin

Acknowledgements

Many thanks to the following people, organizations and government departments who have given their time, energy and resources.

Sue, Bart and David Rayner: for the many informative and enjoyable visits we have shared — the numerous trips to Chantry Island and the lighthouse on the "Rayner Shine". Your continued help and enthusiasm is appreciated.

John Weichel: who has always warmly welcomed us and helped in many ways to make this publication worthwhile. Thank you, John.

Ron Beaupre: for sharing his pictures and knowledge of Lake Huron shipping. Your help was indispensable.

Mr. and Mrs. Bob Stephenson: for the tour of the "Sea Shanty" museum, the sharing of your vast nautical knowledge, and the friendship of fellow researchers.

Malcolm Kennedy: for your time and photographic talents. Your pictures capture the beauty of Chantry Island.

James Bache, Toronto

Bill Tennant, Brantford

Mr. Albert Smith, Tiverton: for providing us with information on the Lambert family.

Jean and Lorne Brown, Helen Clarkson, Ross Bache, John and Donalda Matheson, John Reynolds, Dan McLeod, Pat Saunders, Art Knechtel and family, Andrew Todd, Heather Kinmond, Mabel Huber, Almeda Greathead, Margaret Kitchener and Mac Brown: for graciously opening your homes to us, sharing your pictures and stories of local history. Thank you for the warm feelings and the encouragement.

Southampton Tourist Information Centre, Gladys Thompson and staff: for your continual support and positive attitude towards our endeavour.

Bruce County Museum, Claus Breede, Barbara Ribey, Vicki Cooper and staff: for your excellent research facilities and photographs, as well as the special attention you have given us.

Ontario Public Archives, Toronto

Public Archives Canada, Ottawa: special thanks to Glen Wright and Richard Brown, Trade and Communications Records; National Map Collection; National Photography Collection.

Canadian Centre for Inland Waters

Canadian Coast Guard, Transport Canada, Toronto: special thanks to Alfie Yip.

Canadian Coastguard Base, Parry Sound: special thanks to Capt. B. Sadler and Capt. J. Kennedy.

Environment Canada, Canadian Wildlife Service

Ontario Ministry of Natural Resources

National Historic Parks and Sites Branches, Parks Canada

Burlington Historical Society, Mary Fraser.

Metropolitan Toronto Library.

Wiarton Echo Publishing Ltd., The Beacon Times.

The Great Lakes Historical Society — Inland Seas, Vermilion, Ohio

Trinity House Lighthouse Service, London, England; P.W. Ridgway

To our family and friends, who have continually helped and supported us in our endeavour.

Special thanks to the Ontario Arts Council.

The Saugeen rivermouth provided limited shelter for early schooners. – Bruce County Museum

The tower is entered through a doorway with a circular fanlight over it. There are five runs of straight stairs of 15 steps each, one run of 11, and a curved iron stairway of 9 steps.　　－ Bruce County Museum

This is the story of a lighthouse and its ray of hope. Woven within its walls are the tales of those who braved the buffeting winds, turbulent seas and rocky shoals to scratch their marks on its history.

The Chantry Island lighthouse has long been identified with Southampton. The circular stone structure has been warning mariners of nearby shoals since April 1, 1859.

Chantry Island lies a mile and a half southwest of the Saugeen River mouth at Southampton and is bordered by extensive shoals of massive granite boulders. The island was christened in 1822 by Captain Henry Bayfield of the Royal Navy during his hydrographic survey of Lake Huron. He named it after a friend, Sir Francis Chantry, a noted British sculptor.

The island is a study in contrast. A death-trap to unwary mariners, its reefs radiate like tentacles for over a mile to the north, south and west. Yet Chantry Island provides Lake Huron with a rare protected leeward side, where vessels can ride out even the most violent storm.

To approach Southampton by water has always been difficult. By the early 1850s, Chantry Shoal and the nearby shifting sandbar at the mouth of the Saugeen River had already claimed a number of pioneer sailing vessels. Some of the victims from these early wrecks were buried in the yard of Southampton's first settler, Captain John Spence, and it did not take long for the name Chantry to become synonomous with danger and destruction.

Besides these shipwrecks, a number of other factors pressured the colonial government for improvements in navigation.

Lake Huron was poorly lit. Along the entire Canadian shore of the lake, mariners were wholly unaided by either lights or buoys, with the exception of the lighthouse at Goderich, built in 1848.

With the opening of the Queen's Bush and the sale of the Indian Lands on the Saugeen peninsula, settlers began pouring into the Upper Lakes region and demanding water transportation. Traffic on Lake Huron increased rapidly. Free trade with the United States, in 1854, lifted the duty on fish, furs and lumber, promising prosperity and economic development. The opening of the Sault Ste. Marie canal, in 1855, gave trading schooners access to Lake Superior as well. With the advent of the sidewheel steamer and its increased use at night, calls for navigational aids could no longer be ignored.

To remedy this situation, in 1855 the Department of Public Works contracted John Brown of Thorold to erect the stonework for a series of lighthouses which would light Lake Huron and Georgian Bay from Point Clark to Christian Island. Originally 11 lighthouses were contracted for, but the project was accompanied by such difficulty and expense that only six were completed during the 1850s.

Those on the original contract were:

1) Point Clark
2) Chantry Island
3) Cove Island
4) Griffith Island
5) Nottawasaga Island
6) Christian Island
7) White Fish Island
8) Mississagi Strait
9) Isle St. Joseph
10) Clapperton Island
11) Badgley Island

A lighthouse was never placed on White Fish Island, although one was repeatedly recommended. The last four in the series, marking the North Channel of Georgian Bay, were built years later of wood, by different contractors. They were fitted with cheaper reflectors and flat-wicked lamps, since the cost of the first six far exceeded the original estimates.

The Public Works commissioners wanted an experienced contractor with sufficient capital to finance the steamers, schooners, barges and machinery necessary to complete such towers on isolated sites around the Saugeen peninsula. They could not have chosen a more qualified, dedicated man.

John Brown of Thorold, builder of the Imperial Towers.   — Woodward Grant and Co. Lith.

The year 1809 marked John Brown's birth in Lanarkshire, Scotland. Coming from a poor family, he had little chance to gain a formal education and was soon apprenticed to a stonemason in Glasgow. Lured to North America at the age of 23, his first building contracts were secured in upstate New York. The Niagara Flouring Mills of Lockport and the Cataract Hotel of Niagara Falls, N.Y., soon bore the mark of his chisel.

By 1838 John Brown had emigrated once again, this time to Canada, where he immediately seized the opportunity to open and develop the Queenston Quarry. This was a masterful stroke of planning and foresight, since canal and railway fever had gripped Upper Canada.

Though early contracts were small, such as constructing the bridge and culvert abutments on the Erie and Ontario Steam Railway and furnishing stone for the rebuilding of Fort Niagara, demands for the high-quality stone from Queenston Quarry increased rapidly. John Brown's acquisition soon began to pay dividends. The 40 wooden locks of the original Welland Canal were scheduled for replacement by 27 limestone ones, and the government demanded that stone from the Queenston Quarry be used to the exclusion of all others. Besides furnishing the materials for the locks, John Brown also undertook the construction of several sections of this second Welland Canal.

By 1850 John Brown's reputation and wealth had grown considerably and he had begun to branch out into related industries. With various partners, John Brown opened plaster beds, cement and plaster mills, lime kilns and a steam sawmill. He also became involved in shipbuilding. With such a wide variety of resources at his fingertips, John Brown became the ideal candidate to construct the Imperial Towers on Lake Huron.

Cove Island lighthouse after a new coat of whitewash, November 1948. This lighthouse marks the entrance to Georgian Bay from Lake Huron proper. — Public Archives Canada: PA-143-637

Christian Island lighthouse and keeper's dwelling in 1880.

– Public Archives Canada: PA-143-582

The completion of the contract was to become a monumental task, a matter of principle to John Brown. When construction of the lighthouses began, there were no means of obtaining information about the position or accessibility of these sites except from poorly detailed charts and maps. These gave only faint ideas of location and nothing about the difficulties and uncertainties one would face in these remote wilderness areas.

Work started smoothly with the purchase and charter of a number of steamers, schooners and lifting scows. Quarries were opened at Owen Sound, Main Station Island and Inverhuron. Masons soon began cutting and preparing the white dolomite limestone, which was then loaded on scows and towed to their respective sites. However, at Chantry Island, a breakwater of 540 feet was also being built in conjunction with the lighthouse, and the quarry on Main Station Island could not supply the needs of both. A flotilla of barges, scows and tow boats from Owen Sound was necessary to bring stone for the base courses and the exterior facing of the lighthouse. Cement was brought from John Brown's mill in Thorold.

As well, transportation of men and materials to Chantry Island became a major problem. Enroute to the island in 1855, the chartered steamer *Oxford* was wrecked at the Fishing Islands. A second steamer, the *Mazeppa*, was lost at Chantry Island the following year, and in 1857 a supply tow boat sank in broad daylight when it struck the end of the south reef. These losses are not hard to imagine when one realizes that at this time there were no accessible harbours and no landings were possible except upon the unsheltered beaches of the lake.

Other factors drove up the cost of the lighthouses. Workers had to be paid higher wages to induce them to work at these remote, isolated sites. Storms caused incessant delays, and late delivery of the lighting apparatus kept the men idle. (A lighthouse-building spree in the United States during the 1850s put additional demands on the same Paris manufacturer who supplied the lighting apparatus for the Imperial Towers, causing more delays.)

The lighthouses carried a high price tag. The original contract price, at £3,500 for each tower, escalated rapidly.By the Spring of 1857, John Brown had lost £1,500 on each lighthouse and petitioned the Governor General, Sir Edmund Walker Head, for funds to save him from ruinous loss. (The total price of the six Imperial Towers was $222,563.91, once the cost of surveys, engineering, stonework, lighting apparatus and transportation of men and material were tallied — an awesome sum to a struggling Upper Canada in the 1850s.)

Realizing the importance of the lighthouses, John Brown stated in his petition that he would do everything in his power to complete them, without profit to himself. He took great pride in his work. Samples of his plaster and cement were judged at international exhibitions to be of superior quality. They won medals for him at the Paris exhibition in 1855 and another at London's World exhibition in 1862. This was quite an achievement for the quiet man who lived humbly in a Thorold boarding house for 27 years.

John Brown lived by one rule. Whenever he found a good man, he always endeavoured to keep him in his employ. Some men worked for him for 30-40 years. He continued to complete government contracts until his death in 1876.

After the initial survey, basements were blasted out of the rock for both the lighthouse and the keeper's dwelling. (Local reports state that a connecting tunnel was built between the basement of the light and the house.)

Though inexperienced at building lighthouses, the masons were extremely skilled. Only the best materials

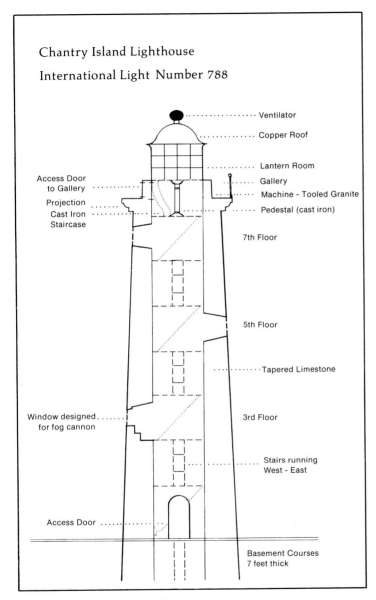

Chantry Island Lighthouse
International Light Number 788

- Ventilator
- Copper Roof
- Lantern Room
- Gallery
- Machine - Tooled Granite
- Pedestal (cast iron)

Access Door to Gallery

Projection

Cast Iron Staircase

7th Floor

5th Floor

Tapered Limestone

3rd Floor

Window designed for fog cannon

Stairs running West - East

Access Door

Basement Courses 7 feet thick

Cross Section of lighthouse.

were used and the limestone was carefully chosen to be free from cracks, so moisture could not penetrate. The foundation of the lighthouse was a bed of cement laid upon a gravel and boulder bottom. The basement courses of rock reached a width of over seven feet. At ground level the walls were fully six feet thick, tapering until they reached the top of the seventh floor, where the walls flared into a projection to provide support for the outside gallery around the light. The exterior stone was squared, even coursed, and hammer faced, while the interior stonework was carefully worked, squared and in broken courses. An entrance archway gave way to a core of cold, unpainted stone with deep-set windows, giving it the look of a castle keep.

The light on Chantry Island took four years to build. Work began in 1855 and the light was first exhibited April 1, 1859.

One of a series, the lighthouse is almost identical in design to those on Point Clark, Cove Island, Griffith Island, Nottawasaga Island and Christian Island.

All were fitted with the latest lens lights from the Louis Sautter Company of Paris. (The International Association of Lighthouse Authorities states that this company has changed its name several times in the last 130 years and finally discontinued the sale of lighthouse optics in 1968, when known as the Sautter Harle Company.)

Though basically identical, minor variations such as window placement were necessary to view approaching vessels. Each one also had a distinctive light characteristic so it could be distinguished from the others. Chantry Island was a fixed light, while others were revolving or flashing.

There is much speculation over the origin of the term Imperial Towers. They were all built under Canadian direction, although consulting engineers may have been British officers. The most likely explanation is that funds from the Imperial treasury were necessary for their completion.

Of the six Imperial Towers completed, only five reached a height of 80 feet (from their base to the middle of the light). The light on Christian Island was only 55 feet (John Brown built a matching 55-foot tower in 1858 at Burlington, Ontario, after sparks from the steamship *Ranger* set fire to the pier and wooden lighthouse on July 18, 1855. The stone lighthouse still stands today, dwarfed by the twin skyways.)

A number of other men played important roles in the construction of Chantry Island lighthouse.

A.G. Robinson was the officer appointed by the Public Works department as engineer and overseer of the Lake Huron lights and harbour improvements. He laid out the sites and inspected the work as it progressed.

Thomas Godfrey, who had served as Superintendent of Lighthouses for the Public Works Department, in charge of teamsters and labourers, was given the position of foreman at the Chantry Island works starting April 1, 1855. He, along with his son-in-law Thomas Lee, had built the first bridge over the Saugeen River, north of Walkerton, in 1852.

Very little work was done at Chantry Island during 1858. Delivery of the lighting apparatus from Paris, France, was delayed until late in the year. Its journey was a long one. The lantern and lens had been manufactured by the Louis Sautter Co. of Paris, then freighted to the Havre by the J.J. Vickers Co., and stored there in the warehouse of M.J. Borst and Co. until transatlantic shipment by steamer could be arranged. It was finally conveyed to Toronto by Francois Baby,' then freighted on the Northern Railway to Collingwood. The steamer owned by the Jones, Black and Co. finally shipped the light to Chantry Island.

When it arrived, a crew of French technicians headed by A. de St. Aubin assembled the prefabricated

The Burlington Bay lighthouse was one of the first in Canada to be adapted for the burning of coal oil, circa 1928.

— Public Archives Canada: PA-88064 – John Boyd

13

lantern room made of cast iron, copper alloys and glass. The interior diameter of the lighthouse had remained a constant ten feet six inches to accommodate this lantern room.

The eighth floor consisted of an iron deck furnished by C. Vale & Co. and was supported on "I" beams and early "T" rails. On this stood a columnar pedestal supporting a cast iron base plate. This fit inside the circular iron gallery around the base of the lantern and formed the ninth floor. Here stood the Argand lamp and Fresnel lens. The lantern room surrounding the light and lenses had to be strong as well as unobstructive.

Since the walls of a lighthouse are thinnest just below the lantern room, they had to be constructed of granite rather than limestone. The origin of this machine-tooled granite provides an interesting mystery. Fires in Southampton and Ottawa in the late 1800s destroyed many original designs and records. Those that remain are incomplete. Local legend claims that some of the stone for the lighthouse came from Europe as ballast for a number of sailing vessels. Although seemingly improbable, it cannot be discounted, since the courses of granite above the projection may have been transported from France, along with the prefabricated parts to ensure the delicate lenses fit properly on top of the tower.

Chantry Island lighthouse has six rectangular windows, each a quarter turn of the tower from the previous one. The window on the third floor poses another mystery. It is recessed to the floor and is fully five feet deep. It may have been originally designed to be fitted with a fog cannon, since explosive gun cotton was used as a fog warning in many early lighthouses. An old stone hut at the south end of the island may have been a powder magazine, although other stories over the years describe it as a lime kiln, an ice house, a smokehouse and a storage shed.

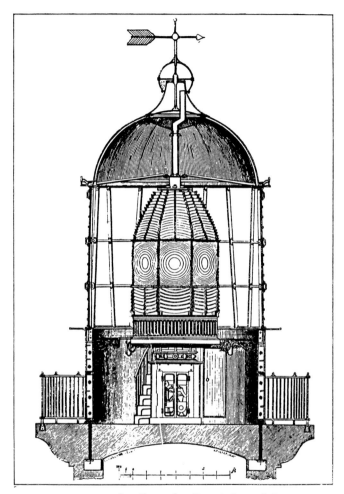

Lantern room and gallery of a dioptric lense light.
– Public Archives Canada

IMPERIAL TOWERS

Name of Light	Height of Light Over Water Surface	Height from Base to Centre of Light	Characteristics of Lights		Remarks (1859)
(A) Point Clark	87 feet	80 feet	Revolving White	2nd Order	(A) This light marks a dangerous reef which runs out a considerable distance beyond it into the lake, directly in the line of coasting vessels; it is readily distinguished from Goderich on the south or Chantry Island on the north, both of these being fixed lights.
(B) Chantry Island	86 feet	80 feet	Fixed White	2nd Order	(B) This light enables vessels to stand for the island, under lee of which, on the east side, there is considerable shelter; but a reef runs out to the S.W., fully ¾ of a mile from the southerly point of the island.
(C) Isle of Coves	90 feet	80 feet	Flashing White	2nd Order	(C) Situated in the strait between the Georgian Bay and Lake Huron; light easily distinguished, vessels pass to the north of it at a distance of ¼ of a mile or more; at about three miles to the north of it is a sunken rock, above which there is only four feet of water.
(D) Griffith Island	130 feet	80 feet	Fixed White	3rd Order	(D) This light, in addition to its other advantages, is of service to vessels making Colpoy's Bay, which affords good shelter and holding ground, from two to ten fathoms of water.
(E) Nottawasaga Island	86 feet	80 feet	Revolving White	2nd Order	(E) This light is situated to the west of the entrance to Collingwood Harbour.
(F) Christian Island	61 feet	55 feet	Fixed White	4th Order	(F) This light is on the S.E. spit of the island and on the west side of the southern entrance to the harbour. This harbour is well sheltered and has a depth of from five to 12 fathoms. The south entrance has a depth of 16 feet, and the two northern ones are from six to 20 fathoms deep.

Late in 1858 the first completed light was exhibited. The schedule of lighting was as follows:

Cove Island	October 30, 1858
Nottawasaga Island	November 30, 1858
Griffith Island	December 27, 1858
Chantry Island	April 1, 1859
Point Clark	April 1, 1859
Christian Island	May 1, 1859

Up until this time, temporary lights had been merely lanterns suspended on mastheads or from poles on the uncompleted towers.

Robert Mills was Chantry Island's first keeper. He kept a temporary light from 1855-1857. The light was merely a seaman's lantern suspended from a mast, and later from a pole on the tower of the lighthouse. During 1857 he received a salary of £127/19/11 and supplies worth £99/10/8 to see him through the year.

GODERICH AND SOUTHAMPTON LINE.

1867   1867

Shortest, Cheapest & Most Direct Route.

THE NEW AND ELEGANT SIDE-WHEEL LOW PRESSURE STEAMBOAT

SILVER SPRAY,

CAPT. D. ROWAN,

Will Ply, in connection with the Grand Trunk Railway, between

GODERICH AND SOUTHAMPTON,

TOUCHING AT KINCARDINE, INVERHURON AND PORT ELGIN, EACH WAY,

DAILY.

Agents for the transaction of FREIGHT BUSINESS

AT THE PORTS MENTIONED.

Tickets for Sale on the Boat for all Points in the Province and the United States.

JOHN V. DETLOR & SON,

GODERICH.

Once completed, the limestone lighthouses were a stark contrast to the low, flat-roofed log shanties of the early Saugeen settlers. Its massive courses of stone and chiselled cornices provided a sense of solidity and permanence.

The original light placed in the bright red polygonal lantern room was a virtually smokeless oil wick lamp, first introduced by Ami Argand of Switzerland. It had a series of tubular wicks, through the centre of which a current of air was drawn up. The free circulation of air produced a flame that burned brightly. A glass chimney also improved ventilation. The flame was of uniform height and remarkably constant.

To concentrate the available light into beams focusing on areas where warning was desired, lenses were placed in frames around the centre lamp. This Fresnel lens apparatus was principally constructed of triangular-shaped prisms and plates of transparent glass. Each was different from the other in its angles, but all were cut mathematically, so that all the rays were bent by reflection and refraction and they became parallel horizontal rays.

These lens lights came in different sizes or orders. Their order was determined by the distance from the centre of the light to the inner surface of the lens. Chantry was a second-order light, a size used to mark dangerous shoals or river mouths. The cutting and grinding of the lenses called for craftmanship of a very high degree. The lenticular apparatus was costly, but required no adjustment once installed. By 1860 there were only ten dioptric lights in Upper and Lower Canada. Six of them were placed in the Imperial Towers, while the other four were located in lighthouses on the St. Lawrence River.

Early steamers would deliver whale oil and supplies for the lighthouse to the Steamboat Wharf (Bogus Dock) at Southampton. Fishermen would then ferry the supplies to the lighthouse.

Originally the circular-wick Argand burners could only burn sperm whale oil. This was delivered in 50-gallon casks to each light station. However, the oil would only remain limpid to 30-40° F, and keepers often complained of a poor quality flame from whale oil they judged to be too old and too thick.

Because of these problems and because of the high cost of whale oil, experiments were made in 1862 with vegetable oil. This Colza oil had to be imported from France and Holland. However, twice as much oil had to be used to get a comparable light, and after a few years, lights were once again fed by whale oil. Sperm oil was last used in 1868, when a new lamp was invented for the burning of petroleum oils in lens lights. Known as Doty's Patent, the lamp greatly reduced the price of fuel for lighthouses.

Chantry Island has used a variety of fuels during its history. Sperm whale oil, Colza oil, coal oil, kerosene, acetylene and electricity have powered the light. Presently it is solar powered.

To keep a constant bright light, proper ventilation of the lantern room was necessary. A trap door in the ninth floor, removable floor panels, a glass chimney and a ventilator in the copper roof provided sufficient drafts to carry off combustion wastes.

On a winter night, ten quarts of oil would be used. For each quart of oil, more than one quart of water vapour would be produced. In a room ten feet six inches in diameter and ten feet high, with glass walls, the cold air outside would cause the water vapour to condense or even freeze, obstructing the light. Keepers would have to crawl out onto the three-foot gallery and scrape ice from the windows in sub-freezing temperatures. Eavestroughs located on the inside took care of most of the condensation. The water drained out through spouts concealed in lions' heads. These were located at the top junction of each of the 12 glass panels, and the water spilled outside. Wrought iron

A second order lens in three pieces on display at Prescott, Ontario in 1914. It is similar to the Fresnel lens used at Chantry Island.
— Public Archives Canada: PA-143-613

handles between the glass panels gave hand holds for keepers to clean the exterior glass.

The plan of the keeper's house shows a large general purpose room across one end, with a fireplace for cooking and heating. This was a living/kitchen area. To the right of the front door was a parlour and behind that a master bedroom. The rooms above the stairs were merely loft bedrooms. Storage sheds, summer kitchens and small barns have been erected at various times on the island.

WRECK OF THE "BRUCE MINES."

EXTRACT of a Letter from a Passenger on board the ill-fated Steamer *Bruce Mine*, describing her loss off Cape Hurd, on Lake Huron, on Tuesday the 28th December, and the miraculous escape of the Crew and Passengers.

"We left Goderich on Monday, 27th; during the night a terrific gale came on, and we sprung a leak; everything that could be got at was thrown overboard to lighten her, but the water continued to gain on us; at daylight it had put out the fires, thus stopping the working of the engines; the rudder had become disabled, and we were perfectly at the mercy of the waves.— At two p m., we could see land from the mast-head, apparently about 20 miles distant, and we were drifting towards it at the rate of about a mile an hour. At ten minutes to three p.m. (when we all hoped she could be kept afloat at least eight hours longer by means of the pumps) the carpenter rushed up and reported that she could not possibly float five minutes longer. There were 26 souls on board, including three passengers and myself. There were only two small jolly boats to save us. A rush was made to them, when Captain Fraser (a son of the late Colonel McKenzie Fraser) produced a brace of pistols, and, cocking them, threatened to shoot down the first man who attempted to get into either of the boats until ordered to do so; this had the desired effect. I was assisted to the mate's boat with fifteen others; the captain took nine with him; the latter's boat was launched without difficulty, but ours getting foul, the tackle could not be let go, and the mate, with wonderful presence of mind, grasped an axe which fortunately was lying close by him and commenced cutting the four parts of the rope, and as he had severed the last the part to which it was attached disappeared below water, and down went the boat with such a crash that, in that fearful gale, it might have been heard two miles off. The "five minutes," in which to make our preparations to leave the wreck, had hardly expired, when the steamer was rapidly sinking in about 70 fathoms of water. Already we had had two fearful escapes, for if the last stroke of the axe had failed to do its duty, we must all have gone down within five seconds; and secondly, if the promenade deck had not parted bodily from the hull, and that prevented the suction, both boats must have been drawn into the vortex. And now our danger was, apparently, as great as ever, for before we left the wreck, the captain and mate had come to the conclusion that the small boats could not live ten minutes in so heavy a sea—the waves rolling mountains high, and we having at least fifteen miles to go to reach the shore. I pulled one of the only two oars in the boat—we of course headed for shore, and I am at a loss to describe the fearful passage in—almost every wave would have filled the boat, but three buckets having been luckily thrown into her, the men were enabled to bail her out in the intervals between the coming of the waves, which were so large that about half a minute would elapse between them About 10 P. M. we got among tremendous breakers, which advised us of our proximity to shore; to the surprise of all we got safely through them, and within a minute after we passed close to the point of Cape Hurd—a most fearful iron-bound coast, and, to our unspeakable joy, a bay of calm water. If we had touched there even one hundred yards further down than we did, we should have been dashed against rocks and all inevitably lost; and that dangerous coast extends about one hundred miles; but it was the will of the Almighty that we should land on the only spot of all that coast where we could possibly save ourselves, and that in the dark. All hands felt thankful. Our mate (Duncan Lambert, of Goderich,) one of the very few men on board who knew anything of Georgian Bay, gave us the unwelcome information that there was not a human being, even an Indian, or an ounce of food within one hundred and thirty miles of us, and that that distance could be accomplished only by boat—that it never could be walked, and if the wind continued we must inevitably starve, for not a pound of anything eatable had we saved. We made a fire, and our all, namely, our clothes, in which we had been drenched to the skin, we allowed to dry upon us. Next morning we walked round the island upon which we landed under the point, and descried with joy a smoke on a neighboring island, which we at once concluded to be that of the captain's party, and which was the first news we had of their having reached land. We immediately made a fire, in order to attract their notice, when they came over to us. We were once more all together again, excepting the carpenter, who, poor fellow, having jumped from the wreck for our boat, and missed it, was swallowed up in the vortex. It was then decided that we should run for this place, (Owen's Sound,) and suffice it to say, that after the most dangerous runs from point to point of the coast, (having weathered even a heavier gale than that in which the ill-fated steamer went down) but feeling that we might perish as well by water as by starvation—the waves washed over us constantly and we never had a dry thread on us —we reached this last night (Saturday) at 8 p. m. (4 days and 5 hours from the time the steamer left us), not having tasted food in that time. Captain Fraser reached here with his boats' crew at 3 this morning; we had not seen them after the first day—my position you may imagine, but I will not attempt to describe.

I have been so fortunate as to find here, to my great surprise, a good schooner bound for my place of destination. I intend embarking in her, and if the ice will allow of her making her voyage, all well—if not, we will, no doubt, return here, if nothing unforeseen happens.

I, of course, saved nothing but what I stood in, and that the suit I left home in. I had lent the Captain my fur coat the night before the steamer left us, and he having, luckily for me, pitched it into his boat, I got it the next morning after we reached shore. Only one of the 26 lost his life, and he, poor fellow, not two minutes before he went down, rebuked me for using an oath to one of the men who was too frightened to let go the fire-tackle of the boat. I shall never forget this, and I hope it will make not only me, but all of us better men.

It was wonderful, and I cannot at all account for it, that I never, for one moment, lost my presence of mind, and was as cool as if I had been a thousand miles away from such a scene; and while I was pulling one of the only two oars to shore, from 3 until 11 p. m., I never lost courage, although every wave dashed in my face, and within the first hour my fingers and legs were set with the cramps, so that I had to be carried to the fire after we had landed, and could not move a limb until my clothes had commenced to steam, and now I feel as well and strong as ever I did in my life—no return of my cough, and having only a bad cold in my head.

I am most anxious that the praise-worthy conduct of the mate, in particular, should have the publicity it deserves, he having saved the lives of 16 of us no less than four times. The Captain, the only one of the whole party, knew the route to a civilized place, and it was, of course, impossible that the boats could keep together in the gales we had to pass through, so that they could both be piloted by one person.

The newspaper account of the sinking of the Bruce Mines.

– Metropolitan Toronto Library Board

Letters of application for jobs as permanent keepers poured in from all over Upper Canada as the towers neared completion. One application stood out from the others. It came from Duncan McGregor Lambert, an experienced seaman sailing out of Goderich. He was one of the early settlers of Bruce County, having fished and sailed with Captain Alexander McGregor at the Fishing Islands during the 1840s. In 1850 he had been elected as constable in Goderich, but by 1854 he was sailing once again, this time as first mate on the steamer *Bruce Mines*.

Following the foundering and sinking of this steamer 20 miles west of Stokes Bay, on November 27, 1854, Duncan Lambert's name became well known — he guided two open lifeboats 130 miles to the safety of Owen Sound. His calmness (and the captain's brace of pistols) had prevented a stampede for the lifeboats; Duncan's freeing of a tangled lifeboat with an axe had saved it from being sucked into the vortex of the sinking steamer, and for four days he had guided the lifeboats, making dangerous runs from point to point around Tobermory to Owen Sound.

Duncan Lambert's actions so impressed one of the survivors that he wrote a letter to the *Globe & Mail* on December 16, 1854, recounting the entire story.

Duncan McGregor Lambert was appointed permanent lighthouse keeper at Chantry Island on April 1, 1858. His annual salary was $435.

For his efforts in keeping a temporary light from 1855-1857 on the island, Robert Mills was moved to the new light on Nottawasaga Island. (As a point of interest, Captain John Spence, Southampton's first settler, served six months in 1858 as assistant keeper at Chantry, receiving $94.80. Jos. Holmes was Duncan's assistant the following year.)

During his years at Chantry Island, Duncan turned the island into a self-sufficient nineteenth century light station. He seeded the island to provide pasture

The lightkeeper's house and sheds. William Lambert is in the doorway. The flag on the shed was presented to the Lambert family. — Bruce County Museum

for a cow, planted fruit trees on its rocky soil, and constructed sheds for storage and additional living quarters. His family stayed year round on the island during the early years, and they fished and mended nets to supplement annual income.

Besides tending lights and improving the property, Duncan acted as government overseer for any repairs or additions to the original 540-foot breakwater on North Shoal. It was a constant battle with the sea; 100 feet was washed away in 1861, leaving the breakwater disconnected from the island. Eventually the pier was raised and lengthened to 650 feet in 1865.

Part of Duncan's job was to lend aid to shipwrecked mariners, and he was kept busy. In the decade after the building of the light, 15 vessels were disabled on the shoals at Chantry. Five were totally wrecked and six lives were lost.

On one particular evening in November 1864, both the schooner *Altair* and the scow *American Eagle* went up on the shoals at the island. Duncan and his family aided those from the *American Eagle*, but only quick action by the crew of the schooner *Lilly Dancy*, who were hove to in the protected lee of the island, saved the crew of the *Altair*.

Immediately after this, Duncan Lambert pleaded with the Department of Public Works to furnish him with a small lifeboat so he would never be left in a helpless position to aid mariners. The department made a wise decision and the Lambert lifeboat aided the rescue of scores of those in distress.

In 1870 John Page, the chief engineer of Department of Public Works, decided to make good use of Chantry Island's natural protection. Since there were no natural harbours along Huron's east coast, it was recommended that Chantry Island become an asylum harbour. A basin or roadstead of ample room to accommodate all vessels needing shelter at any one time was planned. This ideal harbour would have a depth of water sufficient for loaded vessels to ride out storms without touching bottom. Good anchorage and easy access were also important.

They began constructing breakwaters, moorings and piers, enclosing an area of 178 acres, which would provide a moderate shelter with a depth of 15 feet. The building of the harbour improvements took seven years to complete and was completed in stages, as money could be appropriated. The total cost was $300,000.

The breakwater or Long Dock was a series of 30-foot square wooden cribs filled with stone. It was built in two sections; one extending from the island and the other from the shore.

The island portion was begun first in 1871, being an extension of John Brown's original pier. It was extended an additional 1,600 feet by a syndicate of local businessmen. Robert Reid, Robert Walker, Robert Baird and Thomas Adair began the work in 1871 and completed it in the Fall of 1873.

Immediately after this, the mainland portion of the Long Dock was begun, being the responsibility of Andrew Lindsay, Thomas Adair, William Wallace and James Brocelbank. Built in a slightly curved line 1,800 feet long, this portion was carried to within 450 feet of the pier from the island. This interval formed the north entrance to the harbour and was known locally as "The Gap."

The entire Long Dock was completed in 1877. It stood seven and one-half feet above the water line and had wooden planking on the top, forming a boardwalk.

In 1871 the Chantry Island lighthouse was painted for the first time, so mariners could spot it more easily in daytime. The following is the recipe for the whitewash that was used:

Half a bushel of unslaked lime with boiling water, keeping it covered during the process. Strain it and add a peck of salt, dissolved in warm water; three pounds of ground rice put in boiling water, and boiled to a thin paste; half a pound of powdered Spanish whiting and a pound of clear glue, dissolved in warm water. Mix these well together and let the mixture stand for several days. Keep the wash in a kettle and put it on as hot as possible with whitewash brushes.

Additional navigational aids were built in conjunction with this harbour. In 1874 a beacon was built on the tip of the south shoal, south of the lighthouse. It was placed in 16 feet of water and was carried up 40 feet above the water line. It was 50 feet across and octagonal in shape. Vessels could safely sail between

Building the landing pier or "Short Dock" at Southampton Harbour. — Bruce County Museum

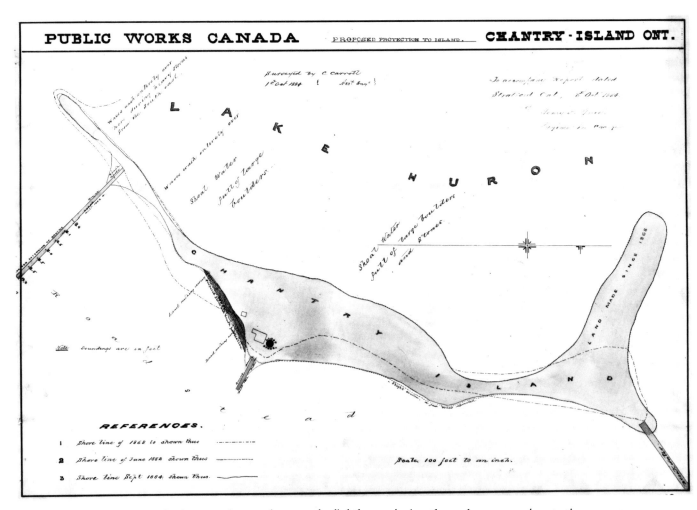

Storms constantly threatened to wash away the lighthouse during the early years and protective groynes were built to ensure its safety. — Printed by permission of the National Map Collection, Public Arvhices Canada

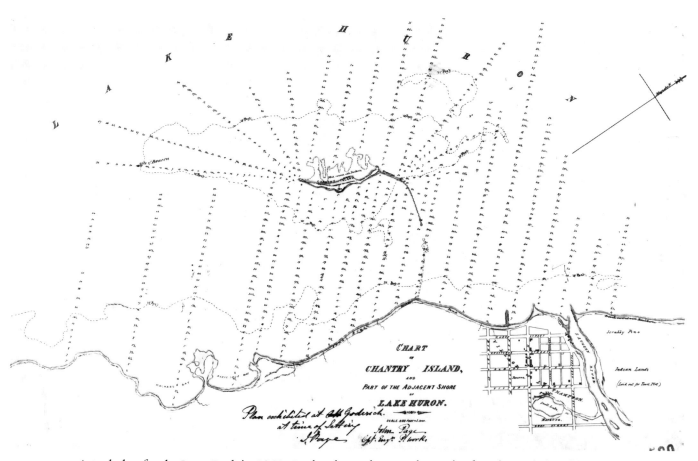

Actual plan for the Long Dock in 1868. It also shows the steamboat wharf on the unsheltered beach at Southampton. It was known locally as the Bogus Dock.

– Printed by permission of the National Map Collection, Public Archives Canada

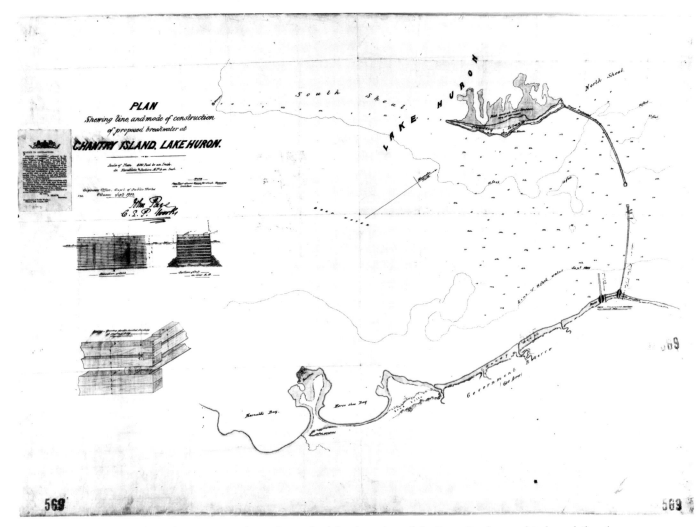

This map of Southampton Harbour shows the island portion of the Long Dock completed, and the plan for the shore portion and landing pier. Also, note the beacon marking the tip of South Shoal. It is dated September 1873. — Printed by permission of the National Map Collection, Public Archives Canada

24

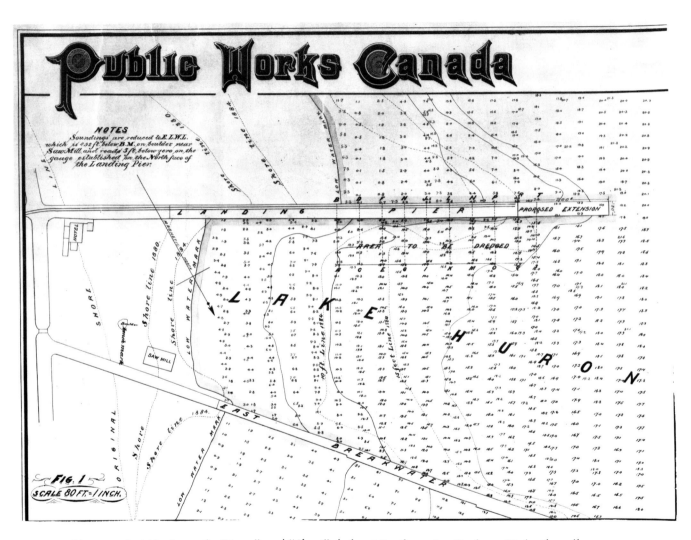

This map of 1889 shows the "Long" and "Short" docks at Southampton Harbour. Notice the railway line of the Wellington, Grey and Bruce extending onto the Landing Pier. The hotel for sea captains be-tween the docks was originally built on stilts. Observe how the piers built up the shoreline over the years.

– Printed by permission of the National Map Collection, Public Archives Canada

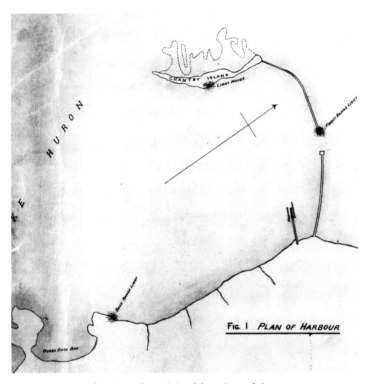

Map showing the original location of the range
lights for Southampton Harbour.
— Printed by permission National Map Collection,
Public Archives Canada

this beacon and the mainland, and this became the
southern entrance to Southampton harbour.

Some 1,500 feet of boulder stone was also removed
from the shoal adjoining the anchorage ground.

In 1877 two range lights were built to guide ships
through the treacherous gap in the Long Dock. The
front tower was placed at the tip of the island section
of Long Dock, being a square, white tower 25 feet
from base to vane. It became the additional responsibility of Duncan Lambert.

The Southampton range light was placed on the
mainland north of Horseshoe Bay, 6,300 feet from the
gap. It was 28 feet from base to vane, a white, square
wooden structure, built in 1877. It was first tended by
David Cascaden. John Lee took over in 1882.

After the turn of the century, this range light was
moved to its present location on McNab Point so it
would more correctly provide a proper line for vessels
seeking the north entrance of the harbour. It lined up
with the front range and the gas buoy on the tip of the
north reef. James Brown took over as keeper in 1904,
and since that time Andy Brown and Jack Buckley
have looked after it.

During 1879 two events took place which marked
the end of Duncan's time at Chantry. First his son
Roland gave up his job as assistant keeper, seeking a
life at sea, and then on September 4th disaster struck.
The scow *Mary and Lucy* struck the south reef at
Chantry during a gale. A yawl of would-be rescuers
was lowered from the steamer *Manitoba*, lying in the
harbour. In it were the first mate of the steamer
Quebec; the captain, first mate, purser, steward and
watchman of the *Manitoba*; and Ross Lambert, son of
the lighthouse keeper. Unable to battle the waves, the
yawl overturned three times during a desperate run
for shore. As the boat capsized for the third time, Ross
Lambert and the purser of the *Manitoba* became
separated from the others. They floated for some time,

The completed Long Dock, Southampton, Ontario.

– Bruce County Museum

A rare aerial view of Chantry Island and Southampton Harbour in 1919, taken from a bi-plane. School registers for that year reveal children were given the day off to visit the plane when it landed.

– Ontario Archives Toronto: S 6211

desperately clutching to a pair of oars, but finally succumbed to the waves of McNab Bay.

The *Mary and Lucy* was washed over the south reef and ran aground on the beach. All hands safely hopped ashore.

Duncan Lambert was broken-hearted and retired from the sea. His second son, William, took over principal lightkeeping duties the following Spring.

Duncan died three years later, in 1883, at the age of 73. He had served faithfully for 22 years at Chantry Island (1858-1880).

A century ago, a lightkeeper's life was filled with security and pride. Appointed to care for only one station, keepers often considered it their home and elected to raise their families there. Tending the light became a family tradition and their children were often hired as assistants. As the parents retired, the youngsters were ready to take over the principal duties. It was never just a job, it was a way of life. The isolation was hard, but many found it rewarding and fulfilling.

On Chantry Island Duncan had, over time, hired two of his sons as assistants — William and Roland. They quickly learned the proper way to remove the canvas covering from the lenses, as well as ensuring that the lenses were clean and level. They carefully replenished the fuel, pumped up the vapour pressure, adjusted the ventilation, trimmed the wicks and adjusted the height of the flame in the burners. It took more time for them to learn how to operate the hand-held foghorn and develop the sixth sense necessary to know when a vessel was approaching. But as navigation closed, in 1879, one of the sons was ready.

William McGregor Lambert was appointed permanent keeper of Chantry Island on April 1, 1880. William was Duncan's second son and was bred to the sea. At the age of eight he was living on Chantry Island, and he became the assistant keeper when he attained his fifteenth birthday.

Duncan McGregor Lambert and his wife, Louisa E. Lambert. Duncan was Chantry Island's first permanent lightkeeper. He served for 22 years (1858-1880).
— Bruce County Museum

29

Sailing through the gap.

– Bruce County Museum

William Lambert and his family on Chantry Island in 1899.
— Courtesy of Jean and Lorne Brown

Drawn to the sea, William became the captain of a sailing vessel at the age of nineteen, the youngest captain on the Great Lakes at that time. Two years later he helped build his own sailing vessel, the *Albionia*, in which he made a record run of ten trips in 11 weeks between Southampton and Detroit, with a cargo of tan bark. During the following years he fished and traded Lake Huron waters, until his father's retirement in 1880.

It was during William's years as lightkeeper that Chantry Island became a showplace. He took pride in keeping a first-class light station and made many improvements to the island. A boardwalk was built from the lighthouse one quarter mile to the Long Dock, along with benches and picnic tables. Flowers, fruit trees and shrubs were planted, making the island ideal for picnickers. Excursions brought people by the boatload to the island. An additional attraction was one of the first marine museums on the Great Lakes, begun by William Lambert, with artifacts he and his family had recovered from the island's numerous wrecks.

Unfortunately, so popular was the island that William was bothered at all hours by people wishing to see the light. Since he had to be up at night to tend the light, he was given permission by the Department of Marine & Fisheries to charge an admission of 10ᶜ to discourage people from viewing the light each time

A leisurely afternoon on the island enjoyed by the Lamberts.

— Courtesy of Jean and Lorne Brown

Day to day life on the island, circa 1880.

The lightkeeper's dock at Chantry Island, circa 1890.
— Public Archives Canada: PA-143-245

they came to the island. As a result, getting to see the light became a special event for youngsters. They were led, one at a time, through the cold stone core of the lighthouse. Once at the top, the lense covers were removed and they suddenly experienced the multi-coloured illumination of the lantern room as the sun struck the prisms. It was truly an unforgettable experience.

During William' time on Chantry, new rules and regulations for lightkeepers were issued. These are but a few of the over 150 items.

Duties of Light Keepers:

1. Lamps lighted at sunset and kept burning at full brilliancy until sunrise. Whenever weather is foggy, lights are to be kept lit as may be necessary for security of navigation.
2. A supply of spare chimneys must be kept clean and ready to replace any smoked or broken ones.
3. In all dioptric lights of second order either keeper or assistant is to be on watch at all hours from lighting up to extinguishing.
4. During heavy gales and stormy weather, no light must ever be unattended by the keeper, except when saving life.
5. Lantern glass is to be kept clean of any obstructions, such as snow, sleet on outside and moisture on inside.
6. All parts of burners are to be kept bright and polished. Other parts are to be perfectly clean, especially air tubes in circular ones.
7. Full-size diagram of the flame as required for a dioptric light is to be hung in light room.
8. Wicks to be lit simultaneously. Glass cylinder should connect with smoke tube to form a continuous chimney.
9. Glass prisms and lenses are to be cleaned every day, being freed from dust by using linen dusters

slightly damp, then rubbed with perfectly dry chamois skins.

10. Level of lenses must be tested. It is fatal to efficiency of light if lense is out of plumb or lamp out of focus.

During his long service on the lakes, William Lambert distinguished himself many times as a lifesaver. He personally rescued a score of people from drowning and assisted others in rescuing twice that number.

Official recognition for these heroic acts took various forms. Following his rescue of Captain Cowell and members of his crew after the sinking of the schooner *Nettie Woodward*, William was presented with a gold watch which bore the following inscription:

"Presented by the government of Canada to William McGregor Lambert in recognition of his humane gallant exertions in saving life on Lake Huron, Ontario, 1st Sept. 1892, and other occasions."

William had battled a full gale for ten hours before finally rescuing the crew, who clung to the mast and rigging. He had been unable to save first mate Joseph Greathead, who had made a desperate bid for shore on a hatch cover, or Nelson Mahan, who died from exposure in the captain's arms.

A bronze medal was his award following his rescue of Captain Joe Glass and crew when the schooner *Cavalier* hit the north reef on the evening of August 31, 1906. This time it was the Royal Canadian Humane Association who recognized his conspicuous courage.

Though never officially recognized, William also had the unique experience of twice rescuing the crew of the schooner *Greyhound*, which stranded in almost identical locations — once in 1889 and again in 1895.

When William retired at the end of the 1907 shipping season, he was presented with the Imperial service medal for 27 years of service at Chantry Island.

William McGregor Lambert, Chantry Island's most famous lightkeeper, with his lifesaving awards.

— Bruce County Museum

Southampton Sunbathers – 1900s.

– Bruce County Museum

Sailing and swimming on Chantry Island.

– Bruce County Museum

Murdoch Matheson's sailboat loaded with picnickers.   – Bruce County Museum

On weekends the steam tug Frank G. MacAulay would be converted into an excursion boat to ferry passengers wishing to picnic on Chantry Island.

– Bruce County Museum

Chantry Island – 1880

Storms of great fury have lashed Huron's shores. In November of 1883, two steamers of the Northwest Transportation Line sought out the Harbour of Refuge during a severe gale. Both the Manitoba and the Quebec went aground just off the reefs of Chantry Island. The tug, John Martin, succeeded in freeing the Quebec which then pulled in behind the breakwater for safety, but the Manitoba lay on the bottom in 7' of water until the following May when it was raised by tugs and pontoons. During the same storm, the schooners Gladstone and the Evening Star were torn from their moorings on the Saugeen River and driven up on land. Three fishing boats were also destroyed and several gangs of nets were lost into the lake. Reports of these wrecks are to be found in the diary of lightkeeper William Lambert.

A sampling from William Lambert's diary.

— Bruce County Museum

1880

March 31	Louisa, Frank, Kate and myself, William, came over to the Island to get the lamps ready to light.
April 3	Light the lamps.
May 5	Moved my family over to Chantry Island.
May 8	Brought cow over in the scow.
July 22	Prop. Arcadia came with lighthouse supplies.
November 8	Took cow over for the winter.
November 25	Moved my family over to Southampton for the winter.
December 5	Put out the lights for the season, Frank and I went ashore.

Money received from parties for seeing lighthouse for the year 1880 – $12.20 (Twelve dollars and twenty cents.)

1881

February 11	Got organ home from W. Bell & Co., Guelph.
March 14	Moved my family over to Chantry Island with Joseph Tranter's team on the ice. Drove cow over on the ice.
April 4	Children, Rossie and Nellie, started to school on the ice.
April 5	Heavy gale of wind with heavy snow from the N.W.
May 1	Light the lights.
July 29	Prop. Dominion came with lighthouse supplies.
August 23	Sir Hector Langevin paid us a visit.
October 11	First frost on the Island this fall.
October 12	Caught 483 herring, first of season.
October 24	Took cow over for the winter.
November 9	Moved family over for the winter.
December 7	Put out the Pier lights for the season.
December 10	Put the light out. Frank and I went ashore for the winter.

Money received from Parties for keeping lighthouse for the year 1881 – $21.00 (Twenty-one dollars)

December 20	Schooner Enterprise left for Kincardine and arrived there.

1882

March 20	Moved my family over to the Island.
March 27	Lit the big lighthouse.
April 9	Lit range light on the breakwater.
July 17	Rossie went to Detroit on Schooner Nemesis.
July 22	Prop. California came with lighthouse supplies.
August 2	Rossie returned from Detroit on Nemesis.

August 29	Found and raised Schooner Ottonobee's anchor.
September 1	Jennie went to Goderich on Steamer Manitoba.
September 3	Jennie returned on the Steamer Manitoba from Goderich.
May 16	Put wire rope protection on the breakwater.

Money received from Parties for seeing lighthouse for the year 1882 – $20.30 (Twenty dollars and thirty cents)

November 4	Pulled the grapes. Cold day.
November 7	Caught 700 perch, net 400 feet long, set five hours at the pier.
November 20	Moved Nellie and Gay over for the winter to go to school.
November 27	Rossie went over to school for the winter.
December 5	Put out the pier lights for the season.
December 6	Put out the light. Dave Benny and I went over for the winter. Caught 45 packages herring.

1883
April 3	Drove cow over on the ice.
April 4	Moved over to Island. I. Tranter's team on ice.
April 13	Took children over on ice. Brought them back with canoe.
April 16	Launched the Peerless.
April 26	Fish boats went out to set nets for the first time.
May 2	Lit the lights.
July 24	Prop. Caltic came with lighthouse supplies.
August 7	Fixed wire rope in breakwater.
October 9	Joseph Greathead came to work. Put up 60 packages herring.
October 12	Prop. Ontario went ashore on Nine mile point.

November 14	Steamer Quebec and Manitoba ashore on inside of the Island.
December 10	Put out pier light for the season.
December 13	Put out the big light for the season and moved over.
November 20	Moved children over for the winter.

Money received from Parties for seeing lighthouse for the year 1883 $10.90 (Ten dollars and ninety cents)

1884
January 15	Sold to Joseph E. Tranter, Daisy the cow for $25.00.
March 6	Moved over to Island. J. Tranter's team.
April 24	Launched the Peerless.
April 28	Light the lights. 30th, fish boats went out first time.
May 30	Manitoba taken off with pontoons and tugs.
June 16	Found Manitoba's big anchor. 21st, found Manitoba's small and quite large anchors.
August 8	Libbie went to her home in Mildmay. 13th, Libbie returned home.
September 10	Found Schooner Dauntless' small anchor. Received $6.00.
October 14	Walter Benny came to work. Put up 95 packages of herring.
November 5	Pulled apples. Very heavy snow storm.
November 27	Moved family over for the winter.

Money received for seeing lighthouse for the year 1884 – $7.20 (Seven dollars and twenty cents)

July 23	Prop. Celtic came over with lighthouse supplies.
December 12	Put out pier light. 13th, put out big light. Walter Benny and I went ashore for the winter.

The journal of a young visitor to Chantry Island in 1899 gives us an interesting insight into the everyday life of a keeper and his family.

5:00 a.m.   – Rose to watch Captain Lambert extinguish the big light and the range light on the breakwater.

6:30 a.m.   – Read a story – wrote in journal.

8 - 9:00   – Breakfasted.
Captain L. took us for a sail in the "Peerless" for an hour or more. Accompanied Captain L. to village to pick up mail and do a little shopping.

12 - 1 p.m.   – Dinner was served.

2:00 p.m.   – Did a little logging – gathered logs that had escaped from boom in harbour.

3:00 p.m.   – Went for a swim.

5:30 p.m.   – After supper accompanied Mrs. and Miss Lambert to light the lamps in big light. The lighthouse is a very substantial tower of quarried and hewn stone 80' high – 100' above water level. The light is of French construction and composed of a series of lenses and prisms so that all rays pass out horizontal.

6:30 p.m   – Meanwhile Captain L. went to light the range lamp and coming back brought Captain Tyson and a sailor from the tug lying in the harbour.

8:00 p.m.   – We sang and listened to solos and recitations.

10:00 p.m.   – After a game of crokinole we retired to bed.

To aid Southampton fishermen, a beacon light was placed at the mouth of the Saugeen River in 1883. It was shown from a lantern hoisted from a mast, erected on a crib 50 feet from outer end of the breakwater pier. By order of council, Murdoch Mcleod was appointed keeper of the beacon August 4, 1883, with a salary of $80 per year. The light burned 44 gallons of oil per year and could be seen seven miles. Donald McAuley took over March 16, 1899.

In 1900 a privately run back range light was shown during the fishing season. It was a green lantern hoisted on a mast 45 feet above water level.

Both of these mast lights were replaced in 1903 by identical enclosed wooden towers. They were 31 feet from their base to ventilator, with sloping sides. Painted white, they showed fixed green lights and could be seen for ten miles. They were built by John McAulay for $1,085.

In 1906 the back range was moved back 1,650 feet and placed on a stone foundation in its present position, 61 feet above the level of the lake.

These river lights have been tended by a series of keepers: John McAulay, Big Angus McAulay, Mr. Granville, John McLean and John McDonald.

Following William's retirement, he was replaced by Malcolm McIver, who continued the life-saving tradition, being awarded a silver watch for a successful rescue. However, town council continued to petition for a life-saving station at Southampton, and on May 7, 1908, the new lifeboat house was opened on the beach near the ruins of the old Bogus Dock. The lifeboat station had a seven-man crew; the coxswain received $75 per year and the crew $2 for each drill and extra when saving life. The drills were very hard work.

The boat was a Beebe-McLellan self-bailing surf boat, built in Collingwood at a cost of $330. It arrived from the Long Point life station in 1907 with full equipment. It was easily transported and launched in shallow water.

In conjunction with other navigational aids, a storm signal drum station was located at the foot of High Street. Baskets of various sizes were hoisted during

The Saugeen River mouth during the 1880s. The mast light and shed are visible at the end of the pier.
– Bruce County Museum

Saugeen Rivermouth after the building of the front range light in 1903. — Bruce County Museum

A view of the Saugeen River at Southampton in 1890, looking east. The storm signal station is visible at the top of the hill. It was later moved to the foot of High Street.   – Bruce County Museum

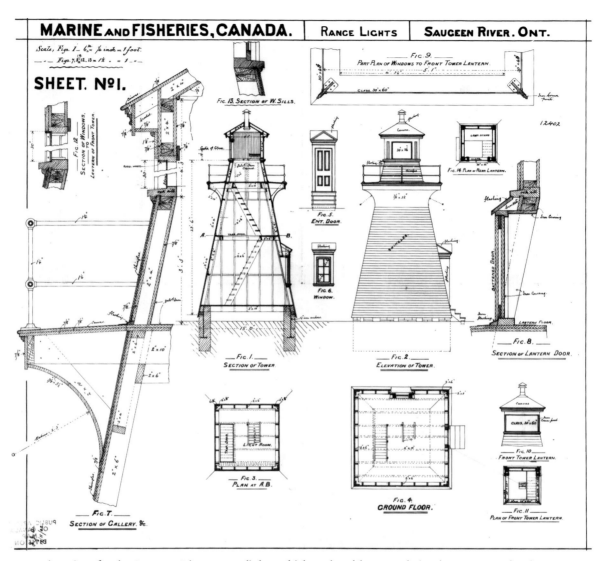

Scale, Fig. 1 – 6 = ⅛ inch = 1 foot.

Figs. 7, 8, 12, 13 = 1½ = 1.

SHEET. N°1.

FIG. 12. SECTION OF WINDOWS, LANTERN OF FRONT TOWER.

FIG. 13. SECTION OF W. SILLS.

FIG. 9. PART PLAN OF WINDOWS TO FRONT TOWER LANTERN.

GLASS. 30" × 60"

12402

FIG. 14. PLAN OF REAR LANTERN.

FIG. 5. ENT. DOOR.

FIG. 6. WINDOW.

FIG. 1. SECTION OF TOWER.

FIG. 2. ELEVATION OF TOWER.

FIG. 8. SECTION OF LANTERN DOOR.

FIG. 3. PLAN AT A.B.

FIG. 4. GROUND FLOOR.

FIG. 10. FRONT TOWER LANTERN.

FIG. 11. PLAN OF FRONT TOWER LANTERN.

FIG. 7. SECTION OF GALLERY. &c.

Blueprints for the Saugeen River range lights which replaced lanterns hoisted on masts. Plan is dated 1902. — Printed by permission of the National Map Collection, Public Archives Canada

The following story was related by John "Kater" Matheson who, as a lad, was forced by circumstances to take his father's place in the life boat. "On Christmas day, in 1917, Southampton residents noticed the lightkeeper wildly waving a flag from the end of the lightkeeper's dock. The lifesaving crew were called out and because his father was out of town, Kater had to take his place. The crew had to struggle with the boat over the snow and ice banks along the shore and row the three quarters of a mile to the lighthouse, often rowing air and slamming into the men in front as the boat battled the icy waves. Arriving at the island they found keeper John Klippert, suitcase in hand, and his little black dog. Fierce storms over the past weeks had prevented them from reaching shore and the only food left on the island was a little flour and water for making scones." John Klipert took problems like this in stride and served as lightkeeper on Chantry Island for 20 years (1917 - 1937).

Southampton's life boat station on the beach. The boat was a Beebe-McLellan surf boat built in Collingwood.

– Bruce County Museum

John Klippert and family during the 1930s.   – Bruce County Museum

storms, indicating wind direction and intensity. Weather instruments originally tended by Duncan were run in conjunction with this signal station. Johnny Trolford looked after the storm signal for years.

The year 1908 brought a series of gales and disasters to Chantry Island. First, on September 5th, the steamer *King Edward* stranded on the island. It had to be pulled off by tugs and towed to Port Elgin. Then, on the evening of October 7th, the schooner *Erie Stewart*, seeking the safety of the Harbour of Refuge, hit the Long Dock 100 yards from the gap. As the schooner broke up, the crew leaped for the breakwater and clung to the lifeline which ran along its entire length. They watched the foremast above their heads shear off and take out the range light at the gap. The crew finally secured a small lifeboat from the hut next to the range light and rowed to the safety of the lighthouse, where they were tended by the McIvers.

The next morning the schooner *Ontario*, looking for shelter, noticed that the three elements needed to find the gap in the Long Dock were missing. The gas buoy marking the tip of the reef was not burning; the range light at the gap was missing; and the back range at McNab's Point was obscured by rain and fog. The captain made the decision to run for the shelter of the river mouth. He avoided the shoals, but fetched up on the gravel bar south of the Saugeen River mouth.

The following week, on October 15, 1908, a new, very powerful 55 ml Diamond oil vapour lamp was placed at Chantry Island. It didn't help the schooner *W.E. Gladstone*, however, which hit the mainland section of the Long Dock and sank on November 23rd.

Malcolm McIver served as keeper at Chantry until 1916. Since that time a number of other keepers have been responsible for its operation and maintenance.

John Klippert took charge April 1, 1917, and retired 20 years later, on April 1, 1937. During his time on the island, the Department of Marine experimented with an early electric light. For a short time after August 31, 1925, it was an unwatched light. However, the experiment was a failure and they went back to kerosene fuel.

Clayton Knechtel took over from him April 1, 1937. He and his family stayed five years, until he took a leave of absence on June 17, 1941, and Alfred Huber was placed in temporary charge.

Lightkeeper Clayton Knechtel (on left) and friend, Clive Morris, on steps of lighthouse.
— Knechtel family

On the opening of navigation in 1942, Cameron Inkster Spencer took temporary charge and was instructed by Clayton Knechtel. After a probationary period, he was permanently appointed August 15, 1942. He served until Chantry Island became electric and a keeper was no longer required, on April 28, 1954. His comments upon electrification were: "No, 'taint shinin' no more, it's just a blinkin'."

The following is a partial list of vessels disabled at Chantry Island and the Saugeen River mouth. Some were total wrecks while others were salvaged. Many other wrecks lie unidentified and long forgotten.

Type of Vessel	Name	Date	Fate
Schooner	*Platina*	November 1848	Wrecked, Saugeen River
Schooner	*Rose of Pine River*	June 1851	Wrecked, Saugeen River
Packet	*Saucy Jack*	November 1851	Wrecked, Southampton
Sloop	*Emma*	October 1852	Wrecked, Southampton
Steamer	*Mazeppa*	November 1856	Wrecked at Southampton
Brigantine	*Sir Charles Napier*	August 1862	Ashore, Saugeen River
Steamer	*Kaloolah*	August 1862	Wrecked, Saugeen
Schooner	*Joseph Wilson*	1863	Wrecked, Saugeen
Schooner	*Altair*	November 1864	Wrecked, Chantry Is.
Scow	*American Eagle*	November 1864	Ashore, Chantry Is.
Schooner	*Anne Hartley*	1866	Ashore, Saugeen
Brigantine	*Fleur de Marie*	December 1866	Wrecked, Southampton
Schooner	*W.B. Hibbard*	November 1867	Wrecked, Southampton
Schooner	*Levi Patten*	December 1867	Wrecked, Southampton
Schooner	*Goldhunter*	October 1871	Ashore, Chantry
Schooner	*St. Joseph*	November 1875	Wrecked, Chantry
Schooner	*E. Fee*	November 1877	Wrecked, Chantry Is.
Schooner	*Mary and Lucy*	September 1879	Ashore, McNab Bay
Steamer	*Manitoba*	November 1883	Ashore, Chantry Is.
Steamer	*Quebec*	November 1883	Ashore, Chantry Is.
Schooner	*Evening Star*	November 1883	Ashore, Saugeen River
Schooner	*Gladstone*	November 1883	Ashore, Saugeen River
Schooner	*Mary S. Gordon*	December 1885	Wrecked, Chantry Is.
Tug	*Alice Brooks*	December 1885	Wrecked, Chantry Is.
Schooner	*Nettie Woodward*	August 1892	Wrecked, Chantry Is.
Schooner	*Greyhound*	July 1895	Wrecked, Chantry Is.
Schooner	*Cavalier*	August 1906	Wrecked, Long Dock
Steamer	*King Edward*	September 1908	Ashore, Chantry Is.
Schooner	*Erie Stewart*	October 1908	Wrecked, Long Dock
Schooner	*Ontario*	October 1908	Ashore, Southampton
Schooner	*W.E. Gladstone*	November 1908	Wrecked, Long Dock
Tug	*A.V. Crawford*	September 1928	Wrecked, Southampton
Motor Launch	*Francis P. Ritchie*	August 1931	Wrecked, Southampton
Fishing Boat	*J.H. McDonald*	January 1934	Burned, Southampton
Steamer	*Islet Prince*	July 1938	Burned, Long Dock
Fishing Boat	*Jackson Bros.*	January 1979	Sank at Southampton

The life saving station at Long Dock, Southampton. The station was moved here for safety after the great storm of 1913.

— Bruce County Museum

The schooner Mary S. Gordon loaded with barrels of salt. It sank at Chantry Island December 7, 1885, but was later raised.
— Courtesy of Ron Beaupre

Southampton. Ont.

This rare photograph shows the schooner Ontario ashore at the Saugeen River mouth October 8, 1908.
– Courtesy of Ron Beaupre

The steamer Carmona, originally the Manitoba, which sank at Chantry Island, November 14, 1883. It was raised by tugs and pontoons the following May.

– Courtesy of Ron Beaupre

The steamer King Edward which grounded at Chantry Island in September, 1908.
— Courtesy of Ron Beaupre

The steam propellers Ontario and Quebec. The Ontario went ashore at Nine Mile Point October 12, 1883 and the Quebec grounded at Chantry Island November 14, 1883.

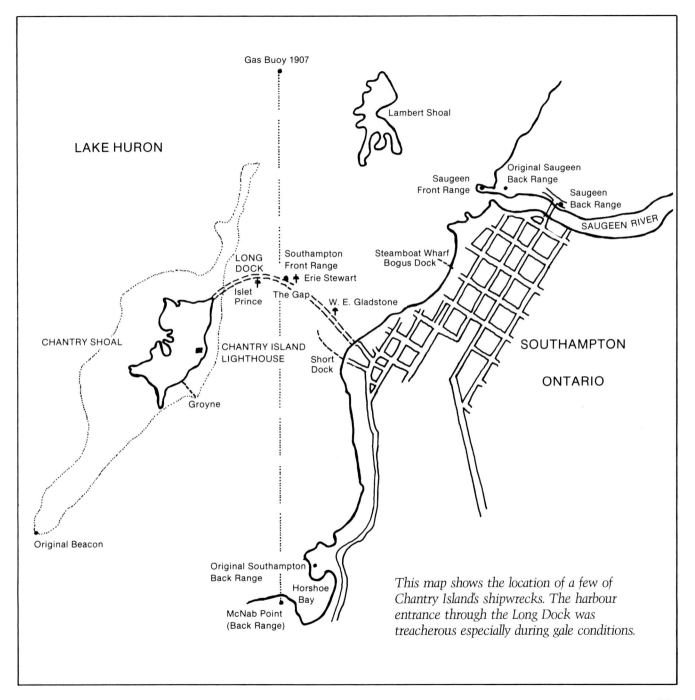

Gas Buoy 1907

LAKE HURON

Lambert Shoal

Original Saugeen
Back Range

Saugeen
Front Range

Saugeen
Back Range

SAUGEEN RIVER

LONG
DOCK

Southampton
Front Range

Erie Stewart

Steamboat Wharf
Bogus Dock

Islet
Prince

The Gap

W. E. Gladstone

CHANTRY SHOAL

CHANTRY ISLAND
LIGHTHOUSE

SOUTHAMPTON

Short
Dock

ONTARIO

Groyne

Original Beacon

Original Southampton
Back Range

Horshoe
Bay

McNab Point
(Back Range)

*This map shows the location of a few of
Chantry Island's shipwrecks. The harbour
entrance through the Long Dock was
treacherous especially during gale conditions.*

View showing Southampton with Chantry Island in the background. — Ontario Archives, Toronto

Birds have always been drawn to the light on Chantry Island. In 1957 the island was brought to the attention of the Canadian Wildlife Service by a group of local Southampton residents and the McIlwraith Field Naturalists of London. They were concerned that the gull and heron populations on the island were being threatened by developers wishing to create a recreational area featuring cottages and picnic areas. The Department of Transport agreed to the establishment of a Migratory Bird Sanctuary, as long as their rights to maintain navigational aids were not jeopardized. On December 20, 1957, the Canadian Wildlife Service had Chantry Island declared a Migratory Bird Sanctuary.

According to the latest census statistics available, Chantry Island has the following population:

7,890 Ring-billed Gull nests
3,797 Herring Gull nests
   70 Black-crowned Night Heron nests
   30 Great Blue Heron nests.

As well, Chantry Island serves as a staging area for waterfowl and shore birds, especially plovers and sandpipers. During migration periods it is a resting and feeding location. Caspian Terns and Double Crested Cormorants, two of Ontario's rare species, use the island during the nesting season.

Since the light went electric, it has been maintained by a series of men responsible for looking after area navigational aids — "Gypsy" Dan McLeod, James Fordham, Fred Rayner, and presently Bart and David Rayner. The traditions of the keepers have continued with these men, and care of the lighthouse has remained a source of pride.

Chantry Island has changed. Storms have swept away its docks and years of sediment have widened its girth. The lightkeeper's cottage now lies in ruins, the victim of vandals, and only the cries of the gulls are left to lament the passing of an era.

Automation has phased out the keepers. No more are hundreds of stairs climbed, lugging gallons of fuel oil, or time spent trimming wicks, adjusting flames and keeping a constant vigil. Light sensors now turn the beacon on at dusk and off at dawn, with solar cells charging the batteries for the electric light.

Only the tower remains unchanged — a limestone monument to those who have served Huron's shore.

A model of the lighthouse and keeper's house built by young Louisa Lambert, of materials found on the island. — Bruce County Museum

Bibliography

Bush, Edward F. *Occasional Papers in Archeology and History*. Canadian Historic Sites #9, 1975.

Canada Department of Marine and Fisheries. Annual Reports.

Canada Legislative Assembly. Journals.

Canada Sessional Papers.

Folkes, Patrick. *Shipwrecks of the Saugeen*. Toronto, Ontario, 1970.

Fox, William Sherwood. *The Bruce Beckons — The Story of Lake Huron's Great Peninsula*. Toronto: University of Toronto Press, 1952.

Robertson, Norman. *The History of the County of Bruce*. The Bruce County Historical Society, 1960.

Stevens, John R. *Lighthouses of the Great Lakes*. Ontario National Historic Sites Service, Manuscript Report #94. National and Historic Parks Branch, Department of Indian Affairs and Northern Development, 1965.

Witney, Dudley. *The Lighthouse*. Toronto: McClelland and Stewart Ltd., 1975.